Driven into the Shade

POEMS BY
BRANDON CESMAT

Poetic Matrix Press
Madera, California

This book was made possible in part by support from the Dorland Mountain Arts Colony.

Published 2003 by Poetic Matrix Press
P.O. Box 1223, Madera, CA 93639

Versions of these poems previously appeared in the following: *Belonging to California:* "Sons"; *Bridge Illustrated:* "Dream Lover"; *California Quarterly:* "River Murmur"; *City Works:* "Beneath Covers," "Californiatown," "Gracias Sabás"; *Comet:* "Park"; *Full Moon:* "Invisible Poem," "Sailing from My Tongue"; *Homestead Review:* "The Conference," "Fingertip Elegy"; *imaginari:* "Lonely Boys"; *inside english:* "Comments on a Stack of First Drafts," "Missile Hat"; *James River Review:* "Driven into the Shade"; *Magee Park:* "Santa Ana," "Shadow Around the Ring"; *no-street poet's voice:* "Suburban Cowboys," "26"; *ONTHEBUS:* "Where Was Fidel When I Needed Him"; *Poetry Conspiracy:* "Poem in Black and White"; *Red River Review:* "Dreaming American," "God Acts"; *San Diego Reader:* "The Long Pass"; *San Diego Writers Monthly:* "Ice Drum"; *Signs in the Landscape:* "The Emptying"; *Teachers and Writers:* "Sliding from Seeds."

Special thanks to Terry Hertzler of Caernarvon Press whose chapbooks "Nightsinging" and "Ice Drum" contributed to this collection.

Book Design by Mary Ellen Wilson of Cavanaugh Enterprises
Printed in the United States of America by The Graphic Overflow

Second Edition

ISBN: 0-9714003-3-4

Table of Contents

Table of Contents continued

To Andie,
whose embrace
is home.

Driven into the Shade

Part I: At Home

GRACIAS, SABÁS

Afternoons, I'd come from the garden
to the kitchen and tell Sabás I was hungry.
My grammy sat at the long table
resting her heart and practicing Spanish with

Sabás who, without burning her fingertips,
turned a white tortilla while it singed brown
and picked up black freckles in the iron skillet.

I studied the tortilla as butter melted, settling its flour-dust
and wished for beans or meat; however,
Sabás gave only this calientito,
nothing more to spoil my dinner.
I don't recall much about the salads, roasts or puddings;
but those tortillas held my afternoon hunger so that

today I look at flour tortillas as topographical maps,
brown and black hills in the white desert,
where masa harina rose into the palms that made them.
I read those circular maps as I put them to my lips,
hoping to trace the ways to Sabás, Ana, Chona or Beatrice,
but the tortilla only leads the way to its edge,
not to the hands that made it,
though many California children would follow
this map to the women who raised us,
would follow from hand to mouth to memory.

SANTA ANA

At my birth, this dry wind wrapped me in
sheets of heat drifting off the desert.
I know before this wind comes:
one last silence
before desert air gusts the dust and smog
west into the sunset,
promising Red Tide in paradise,
threatening brush fires.
Summer blowing into Fall, into Spring, into Winter,
through the houses developed on mesas.

Above the sound of rustling oaks
you can hear complaints about the weather.
Jammed on I-5 for two hours, neighbors pull their guns,
crazy as the wind pushes around them.

At 2:10 p.m., 40 Celsius on empty September streets,
still except for blasts from air-conditioners,
we hold our breath before Summer
blows into Summer; brush flames up canyons
to backyards, melts garden hoses.

Indoors, a real estate broker and an Ohio tourist chat,
but the weather is not a polite subject.
A palm frond blows against a power line
showering the sidewalk with sparks.
Bad for business, the broker thinks.
They lick their lips
as if they're waiting for a kiss,
and blow by blow, we get what we deserve,
blow by blow. I've heard
acorns drop on the fallen leaves,
a sound like big rain, deceived in this desert.

HIS FIRST POEM

The I is another
so much the worse
for the wood that finds out
it is a violin.
—Rimbaud

The jazzed melody of "Buffalo Gals" wrote his first poem,
Dee dee-dee dee, dee-dee, dee-dee dee dee,
his grampy singing songs with forgotten words.
The story of the grandson asking,
"Dee-dee-dee some more, Grampy,"
told every holiday so that everyone believes it.
It's a story about colic and how a father was gone,
how a grampy stayed up through the night,
a story you have to sing to tell.

The boy wrote his first poem on the wall
with a pen he took from an adoptive father's desk.
The boy's first poem appeared beneath the light switch.
The poem said, "OFF."
He began at the end and fought the feeling that
everything that mattered happened before he was born.
The wall switch wrote his first poem
and left his first audience unhappy.

Except for certain pleases, thank-yous & I'm-sorrys,
most of what he said is forgotten.
The boy took to writing lines in the dirt,
riding a horse on trails into the hills.
He lamented the earthmovers on the edge of wilderness.
We destroy creation to increase our faith.

He cultivated syntax to articulate his misanthropy;
daily bread proofread and edited the business letters.
The songs remembered the words.

Meaning will come back with the buffalo.
He watched species extinguished as fast as Adam named them;
the streetlights, illuminated signs and security lights
whitewashed the night; every newborn wiped away a star,
the same stars the preacher cited to him as evidence of God.

SHADOW AROUND THE RING

Father makes us weary on this mountain
so tall the clouds bruise against the summit.
Yesterday, he made us cut branches off a
white fir that fell in last month's snow. We
set these branches around the stone ring for bedding.

Last night in the hard, smoky cold, I woke
twice and saw him poking coals and feeding
another split to the flames. When he looked at me
the corners of his mouth lifted and then fell before he turned
to the dark, as if he too were tired of being with people.

DRIVEN INTO THE SHADE

One Saturday morning after their divorce,
my dad drove home in a new Ford Maverick for Mom.
My little brothers were inside watching "The Bugs Bunny-
Roadrunner Show." I was in the driveway, watching Mom
hang her clothes on a pole above the back seat as if
each dress were one of her possible lives.
Dad pulled me under the oak at the side of the driveway
where the leaves' spindles jabbed my feet.
"Don't cry," he said. "She's going to get some rest."

When we came home from school, we often found her lying down,
the curtains drawn. Her back hurt, she said.
Like a princess she could feel the .22 pistol under her mattress.
This woman who had gentled horses and carried king snakes off the road
wept daily. Her medication, she said, made her emotional.

Now wearing sunglasses, Mom carried her make-up case to the car.
She saw me in the shade with Dad and said,
"You promised you'd take the kids from me. Now you have them."
I threw my arms around her legs so she couldn't walk.
I wanted to make them stay. Instead I made her say,
"Don't make this hard." I made her pull my arms off her and
felt her need to leave, and it was stronger than me.
She said, "I'm no good anymore."
The sand where she stood burned my feet.

Two weeks before, we had passed Dad driving up the road;
she swerved at him and said, "If you kids weren't in the car—"

Now Dad would be safe with us, but
Mom was leaving, so when she went in the house for her purse,
I jumped into the car and locked the doors.
The keys swung in the ignition.
My father told me to open the door.

I shook my head "no,"
my reflection on the glass over his face.
I was no good, whole family no good:
Bad Dad, Bad Mom, Bad Boy.
"You're going to get spanked," he said through the glass.
Mom came out and told him to break the new car's window.
"My gun is in there."
Why would I want her gun? For that moment,
I brought my parents back together outside her new car.
Dad sighed and lifted a chunk of granite from along the drive.
Mom looked at me. With the windows up, the car had grown hot.
I said I'd turn the key and touched the ignition,

but instead of holding them there, I made her turn
on him and say, "You almost had me, almost had my kids."
Dad dropped his stone, and stepped back, his face already blurring
in my memory.

I knew my mother despised his lust for other women and
that I was supposed to hate that part of him and never be unfaithful.
Again he walked down the road, and I told Mom to go indoors.
Outside the windshield and behind her sunglasses, she began to cry again
and promised not to spank me or drive away.
She held out her arms and asked me to open the door.
I was inside the glass.
I was eleven years old.
I had the gun and her medicine bottles.
I had the keys to a new car
pointed down the driveway, but
that moment to leave came too early for me.
I would not open until she went indoors.

One night years later, I drove along a valley above Provo
and swallowed the Quaaludes a woman gave me.
She had calm brown eyes.

We sipped tequila and orange juice while she told me her screenplay
about a woman who works her way home playing soprano saxophone.
I told her a story about a boy trapped in a car.
She laughed and pulled me out into a field where I remembered that,

after my father walked around the curve in the road,
I unlocked the Maverick's door and
stepped onto the sandy driveway. My feet burned,
but cool air stung my lungs and the light off the leaves winked
as I ran for the shade.

HIS NIGHT IN THE VALLEY

Summer's end midnight,
    a boy shivers in a blanket.
The pond below the bluff
    holds yesterday's heat.

A can of beans for tomorrow sits
    by the cold fire-ring stones
while he huddles
    frightened of brush fires.

        In the next valley, his mother watches the late show
        and waits for him to come home,
        but when the credits roll, she clicks off the t.v.,
        the screen collapsing into one dim dot.

Near the muddy bank
    a paw snaps a stick.
Crickets count heartbeats double time.
    Stars poison his eyes.

Summer's end morning
    boy shivers in a blanket.
In the mist over the pond
    floats yesterday's heat.

Part II: Leaving the House

MERCY

apologies to Buddy Guy

Woman
comes in   where I am writing.

Sly lines,
slow smile.   My blood starts a-cookin'.

Thigh touch,
long sigh.   Words start to blurring.

Ear kiss,
mind slips.   I don't want to need you.

What is it about the time she steals,
tumbles my walls, the way I yield?

She pulls me right out of my head.   The room starts to curve.
She hooks my legs so I can't stand.

Take my work from me.
Break my mind finely.
Got me beggin' for mercy.   Mer-cy!

THE LONG PASS

On the football field, some fight, others run away
after the long pass. For all the shoulder pads' clatter and
helmets' crack, football is less culturalistic Darwinism than
a complicated game of catch.

People who love me have always done so in spite of my desire
to hit and shove with or without pads, on grass or sand or mud
as long as the light holds,
                                        the light necessary not to illuminate
the lineman who could dance like a dozen sumo wrestlers in the dark.
No, we light stadiums because football is a game of sky.

When I played tight-end—a halfway-house position for lapsed
                                                                                pacifists—
most of the game I would swing my forearms, throw my shoulders,
and drive my legs into the man across from me.
I was yell, muscle, grunt and rumble.

But for a few plays, I would release from the line and run downfield,
trying to put distance between myself and everyone. It felt good to be
                                                                                        alone,
pray the ball would drop over my shoulder and into my hands, as soft
as I could make them, hold on tightly and run as far as possible.

For all the yelling, I learned to listen for football's quiet.
The long pass flies silently, is no "bomb" unless dropped.

The long pass is a prayer with answers.

After the ball's snap,
the charge of the line and
calls to put the quarterback in a sack,
                    the spinning oblong sphere brings a hush.
                         So much can go wrong between
                              your hands and mine.

The linemen lean back from one another as the ball reaches the apex,
and even drunks in the bleachers quiet as the ball starts to drop
into that moment when we all lift our eyes and together take a breath.

26

Rigoberto Lopez Perez will always be twenty-six
ever since September of '58 when
Luis Somoza inherited Nicaragua.

With twenty-six years, two sons and a vote,
I see mercenaries take office.
Seems Congress re-read the will last night and
Nica belongs to an insurance exec in Miami.
Am I an assassin?
Am I a soldier?
No.
I am a coyote howling at the moon on another night.
Listo y loco, I read too much.
Others call from downtown, but I seek my revolution within
and grow hoarse just before dawn.
No sleep for me while Rigoberto rests.

Somoza Garcia left Managua the silver lake;
Rigoberto left the second stanza to
the poem Nica writes.
To my sons I sing for the americaS,
but only God lives long enough to
hear the whole song.

DREAM LOVER

The first night she pushed him away,
she said, "Let me sleep." How awful to
have dreams so sweet. She slept half the day.
He became jealous of her shut eyes and
watched her by the light from the hall.

She began to frown during afternoon naps with the children.
Mornings, gravity pulled strong on her shoulders.
Nights she read paperbacks.
One day while she walked to the mailbox,
he flipped the mattress, but she never
let on that she felt the difference.

He waited tables during dinner at the Country Club,
then drank draft beer and played the piano surrounded
by tables set for breakfast until his eyelids got heavy,
then he hurried home to lay down before the sun rose.
She came to hate the sight of him on the couch in the morning.

During an afternoon nap, she saw him
leave for the club, walking with his eyes closed.
The bastard had slept into her dream!
He let the kids out of the front yard, and
her legs were too stony to run down the street.
"Do whatever," she told him. She believed he rolled
his eyes beneath their lids, but who knew for sure?

CALIFORNIATOWN

Valley silt over granite, oranges drop and
mold in leaves like clouds blurring the sunset,
the neglected oranges as tart as an anger not forgiven but engendered;
their acid leeches over the reach of roots holding Valley Center.

This is how to taste California, the developing rot like wine going bad,
dry orchards and planned communities confirming the future tense
of old men's dreams for the sunlight.
A Oxacan, wings sweat through his T-shirt,
slices away chemise and ceanothus that hush the dust.
Oranges parceled into wedges garnish hash browns.
Stolen water pumped over the hill.
Every afternoon black rivers of freeway frozen with
parked cars, like Evelyn Mulwray's in *Chinatown.*

Stand on a hilltop clearing and see the weary red eyes of the school bus.
In the evening, sit on any patio and hear tires scream for speed
as parents commute home from San Diego or Irvine,
the next investors to lose money at stolen Warner's Springs
where Escondido and Vista suck down the San Luis Rey River.
How many will move here, blind from snow, west-destined
to miss the oranges rotting and the raven rocking on the phone line?

PARK

At the class reunion, we stand around like a city,
everyone a building, except me, of course.
I am a car and I drive the streets between them.

I feel nostalgic about this old town. I could tell you
the history on most of these buildings. See this high-rise
office? Virgil works here. Someday he wants to own it.

Next door his wife Gloria manages the apartments.
The tenants live quietly and pay their bills on time,
not like their neighbors in Ramon's complex

where someone left the water running in a ground-floor unit,
so the tenants had to move upstairs. Around the
corner, Maureen dwells in an old house that she restored by

pulling back the dusty carpeting from
the wood floors. She likes to keep them shiny,
so they throw the light back where it comes from.

I could drive around all night. Some buildings you can
glance through the front window and tell how things are. Some houses,
we could drive down the alley and look through back windows,

but tonight we don't need to see what goes on in those rooms.
On this cul-de-sac, for example, lives my high-school sweetheart
and wife. See the mansion she's built and the guesthouse to

the side. I'll just wave as we roll past the driveway and continue
on the worn dirt road that drops off the mesa at the edge of town.
See? Nothing but brush, the river and this car with its lights off.

If I weren't such a car, I would build my home here
beneath the edge of the glowing sky,
a garage in the open space beyond the outskirts.

GRAND TRIO

I. Concert

His assistant slices the maestro's veal
and opens the bottle of pinot noir.
The wild rice pilaf threatens no one.

During the season, the public forgives
neither paper cuts nor hangnails. Maestro
walks but never works in his rose garden.

The grand sits on stage, beside the bench.
In the wings, the maestro removes gloves,
hears murmurs until the house lights dim

and stage lights glare on the ebony.
The public—unforgiving as it is—applauds until
maestro sits at the grand to make it sing.

The opera-box view reveals hammers
and dampers leaping and pounding under
the open lid, as well as pale hands

gliding across the keys, black on white,
white on black, over and over. Maestro
raises a hand for those in the back rows:

perhaps a high note in a slow passage.
Otherwise his movements retain symmetry:
maestro's hands, the horizon; the rising

red felt hammers, suns falling onto
bronze rivers and beating them
into arpeggios as hard as clear light,

maestro's flowing hands fooling all,
save those in the opera box, from the
percussive nature of the grand piano.

In rows they stand and clap their hands,
expecting an encore. As if anticipating,
the piano strings quiver in the ovation.

By morning, however, the grand is covered and
closed in a dark, silent room backstage, and
an assistant slices maestro's grapefruit.

II. Baby

The woman of the house had the moving men
place the piano first by the fireplace. She
stood back and said, "Too large together."

Because they couldn't lift the fireplace,
she had the piano placed before the window and
three discs set down sparing the carpet damage.

The way the mahogany plane led one's view
outside to grass, sand traps and flags
under a blue sky beguiled the eye.

Yet as it was, the baby grand appeared barren
until she set a vase of freshly cut irises and
a fan of *Ranch & Coast* on the lid of her piano.

For her parties, she hires pianists who play
Cole Porter and movie themes: vague memory music
twinkling just above the level of hearing

while ice clinks in glasses and tongues rumble.
After three bourbons the colonel wants to sing.
With the guests leaning around the baby grand,

he leads them in a medley of society songs.
A waiter hovers to see that all of the guests
have coasters at the elevated coffee table.

Only a CEO's widow remembers all the lyrics
to "Mack the Knife" and "New York, New York."
She sings verses solo while all have a splendid time.

The colonel's voice nearly sparkles
as the pianist plays warm chords on baby
out of tune, out of place before the window.

III. Upright

In the bar's din, the bass rumbles below
the level of conversing in a conscious sense;
still, a woman taps time, foot to wood,

and shouts across the table. While others to others
reply, the player pounds chords on the keys,
some of the ivory chipped away to gaps of wood,

some stick uneven as teeth in a derelict's mouth,
neither smile nor frown but wrinkled at the edges
by cigarette burns and water ring blemishes.

Ice melts in three bourbon rocks set up after
boogie-woogie, barrelhouse, blues, stomp, rag.
Fingers pump perpendicular; playing with his arms,

using his shoulders, he demands volume with what
seems like violence, but the sound is civil compared
to his daylong pounding on nails with hammers.

In night's inversion, this sunburned man's
fingernails click on keys and he beats out
live music, set up with bourbon rocks or not.

And he says so when his voice escapes from him
thinking no one hears as the singing mixes
with other voices seeking the mob's center.

He gulps cold bourbon and chews ice for his voice,
shuffles home to rest, leaving the upright leaning
between wall and floor, resonating in quartertones.

GOD BOX, 1994

As I've been saying, Brother-Sister Citizen,
he knows the pieces of my heart,
the chambers of desires and floors of piety.
He broadcasts the wrath of shareholders.
He reveals visions of judgment in living color I can believe in:
Oliver, O.J., Hillary and Nixon, Nixon, Nixon.

One of these things is not like the other.
Careful don't let your biases show.
The media's liberal, turn on the God Box
and it tells you that it is so.

Persons unknown interrupt this broadcast of situation comedies and dramas — in which the characters lead lives so interesting that they never watch T.V. — to bring you revelations of new and improved strength . . .

He has delivered unto us commandments and mandates.
Lift up our people on a sea change.
How long, lord, have we waited for a high tide
to raise our boats from the muck of the harbors
and carry us on a course charted in 1950?
Verily, verily, spokespeople say unto us,
"Judge not the righteousness of covert action
lest ye your-own-damn-selves be judged."

The God Box lays me down in green pastures,
rolls me into the Valley of Death,
holds the Angel of Light in my eyes,
never to shine on the Elusive Prince of Peace,
his dove-loving ass no where on the satellite.

Embrace the black and white of Rodney's uncut arrest.
Wrap your arms around our lord
and carry him safely through the shop window.

Kill Connie Chung and all other bearers of bad news;
if Republican women don't mind form over substance,
who are we to liberate bitches from their leashes?
Thank you for the blessing of daytime dramas of wives and
husbands in love . . . but not with each other.
Spare us the family values in broken homes.
Smite welfare and get the widows and orphans off their asses.
Make someone else fishers of fetuses;
let them fill our nets, our schools, our arcades,
and every tract home and prison cell we build for them.

Kneel before the God Box,
lay your hands upon it!
Let the spirit of the airwaves edify you:
the omniscience of George Will,
the omnipresence of satellite and a thousand channels of blight,
the omnipotence of professional sports spanning the globe,
beam it up, lord.
May you find us contrite on easy chairs and couches,
Tuned-in and righteously ascendant on the airwaves.

America, America!
God Box, reveal to me
the country as it ought to be
in 1953.

THE LONELY BOYS

I'm tending bar on a rainy day when
Sean and his grading crew stop by.
The rain falls as if it has been waiting all winter,
holding itself back. We lean into the bar from all angles.
I suggest Irish coffee. Sean declines a second round,
says it's a good day for porno
with the wife at work and
the kids at school.

One at a time, never in twos, the crew leaves the bar.
As I scrub their glasses,
I remember the field behind my hometown market
where Donovan found *Galore* with its photos of
men and women clustered like a DNA strand.
In the field we looked and I wished
first to be the men in the photos,
then to live long enough to lose my virginity,
then to close the distance between me and humanity,
Donovan standing closest by.

We brokered an arrangement:
I'd let him if he let me.
At the end of the afternoon,
my carnal curiosity died to the knowledge that
anal sex is more engaging in theory than in practice.
In other bars there are other theories.

I clean the glass on the aquarium over the back bar and
watch the fish swim for position.
They mirror the customers who swim in
the drinks I mix. Sometimes they drift
into positions of comfort.
I give them what they order,
fill the glasses,
set them on napkins,
step back,
hope they know how to swim.

WHERE WAS FIDEL WHEN I NEEDED HIM?

to Elian Gonzalez

Because your father looked nervous during his interview with the INS,
your granduncle's attorneys don't believe you should go home,
they say your father doesn't really want you,
that Fidel makes him say such things.

When I was six, my father was across the ocean, too.
Divorced from my mother, in arrears for child support,
he'd gone to Vietnam to hide from the court and research how the
communists brainwashed people out of the comforts of exporting rubber.

When I turned 16, I met him. He took me
to a Baja bar where I listened to his voice
as I tunneled beneath our wasteland of memory,
trying to resupply our love, but
the tunnel didn't lead that way.

Throughout the afternoon, he uncoiled his story
how my mother and grandparents hid me from him.
Later his story wound back on itself like a python,
how he drank in Saigon, drank at San Diego State,
drove around Berkeley with a Marine friend
yelling "faggots" out the window at the longhairs.
I could not hear myself in his voice.

He said we were alike because we played football,
but despite the distance between us,
he'd never thrown one pass to me, nor
had I been close enough to lean against him in a block
and feel him push back.

How I wish Fidel had walked into the bar,
taken my father at gunpoint,
locked him in Cuba's darkest prison
without rum and brainwashed him,
electrified the genitals I came from,
made him scream that he wanted me with him.
Where was Fidel as my grampy sang me to sleep,
where was Fidel as my father bought Saigon Tea
for the mothers of dust?

Part III: Collisions

ALL ABOUT YOU

Forgive me for being contrary, but some things
must be said. The sky is falling, while the earth

pushes us forward, so as for the expanding-universe theory,
I offer our lives as counterpoints.

Who can deny that it all is collapsing? Sleep bows our heads;
we must submit even to dream dreams, then the heavy awakenings.

Haven't you felt the weight across the shoulders, the gravitational
force of the heart developing into a black hole from its ingrown

blooming since our arms first drifted into the embrace of
shoulder sockets and legs flew up into our hips?

So now we bind, a collapsible population.
The weakest point in the universe is my hometown in So Cal

where no one can turn around without bumping into
the consequences piling up at the base of the mountain.

You roll your eyes. Would you turn them inward to reveal
facts to the contrary? Or is that your universe closing in?

I would surrender to your gaze and throw myself in would it not
add to the pressure of everything rushing toward you.

GOD ACTS

In Vista, there's an insurance salesman who won't write policies
against acts of God for religious reasons.
But if a river washes away the home built on a flood plain,
that is not an act of God.
If a California quake shakes your house to basin silt,
that is not an act of God.
If *tukwut* hunts you in the Cuyamaca Mountains,
that is not an act of God,
though God no doubt comes through cracks in weather stripping.
His acts are sleep promises made, never touched
like fingertips tracing the hawk's helix.

I will not drive through L.A. during daylight
when freeways chew chunks of people's lives.
I love to fly through the town at night,
the window rolled down, the scent of exhaust faint,
and follow a handful of taillights like demon stars.

At the 5/101 change, just before hurtling through the slot beneath
Alameda Street,
I look at the lights, thousands of them against the dark.
Every morning downtowners get up as if they have a chance,
but even if we all drove to the suburbs,
our back seats full of unmarked bills,
we could only buy another lot to attach to the fray we build.

Housing starts don't clear classrooms of warehoused children who
boost the economy by watching the god box before shopping the mall.

Meanwhile, boys at the Tropicana work out knots built into biceps
while "girls, girls, girls" get even. The cruelest give birth.

California is a landfill for everything that rolls west:
    the gray water of Mission Bay when gravity enforces the law,
the sand slipping off beaches, and the security gate's click;
    in California, these are the acts of gods.

FINGERTIP ELEGY

From where did the muddy tumor in our father's mind roll?
They first found nodes clustered like grapes in his lungs.

Surgery clears the seizures that landslide through his body,
but it also removes the keystone of his brain.

His smile dissolves like adobe brick.
Food rolls into his mouth, a bay at high tide.

He scars his voice with apologies.
To my brother and mother he messiahs his mind.

The doctor scans the stairs of his body. The bones
become like wood grain with seams to split;

the building blocks of his bones topple;
the web of his veins disentangles.

Into the front pew my youngest brother glides with the sin of anger.
Our mother fingers the small hill beside the boy's spine.

People he keyholed applaud the triumph of mud;
a choir slides forward,

and I play "Amazing Grace" on a stone piano
in our iron ritual of grief.

MISSILE HAT

The Pope, John Paul, floats into my comp class,
    the robe, the grace, like Liberace across a Vegas stage.
    Those guys know how to dress.
He sits at a desk beside Esperanza and her son Pedro
    who colors in college because his father comes home at seven.
Just as I'm showing how subordinate clauses rule the world,
    el papa leans over and whispers to Esperanza,
    "You are not alone.
    Children are the blessing of the poor. God is their father.
    Blessings, blessings, blessings," sings John Paul,
    raising his right hand but asking no question.
The class sits rapt. None of my lectures has lit their eyes as
    John Paul does when he says, "No reading. No essay.
    We must visit L.A., mass for the multitude."
    He lowers his hand. "You are dismissed."
They follow him to the parking lot where even Ricky with
    three tears tattooed beside his right eye kisses el papa's ring before
    John Paul ascends and arcs north with aerodynamic ease.
The wind breaks the vapor trail into a miracle:
    a cloud like a jagged scar, a stigmata in the smog.

GUATEMALAN FIRES

Bishop Juan Gerardi
Bishop Juan Gerardi
Bishop Juan Gerardi
his name hard to read:

In Guatemala, Bishop Juan Gerardi's name
burns with bodies of 200,000.   So, counting can kill.

How much fire does it take to   The forensics of boredom,
collapse evidence into ash?   so much factual noise.

As silences go, the frequency of atomic orbits is
lower for dead than for the living.

What do we resonate with?   Who is "we," traveler?
Fire to skin?
Stone to bone?
Dollars to bullets.

Soul rustling:
Tissue of intention.
Fabric of acts.
Friction from smoldering conflicts of interest.

Stumble footnote to footnote,
pitch in the paper names that whisper our history:
Who is "our," traveler?
Beadle Smith, Under Secretary of State in 1954 and board member of
United Brands;
John Foster Dulles, Secretary of State in 1954 and lawyer for
United Brands;
his brother, Allen Dulles,
Director of Central Intelligence Agency in 1954 and lawyer for
United Brands;

Thomas Cabot, President of
United Brands;
and his brother, Henry Cabot Lodge, U.S. ambassador to the
UN in 1954;
John Clementz, Hearst news executive in 1954 and publicist for
United Brands;
General Castillo Armas, dictator, overthrew the elected president of
Guatemala in 1954;
Rios Mont, dictator during height of
Guatemala's genocide in 1980s;
Ronald Reagan, President of
United States, restored military aid to
Guatemala in 1980;
Col. Disreal Lima Estrada, conspirator in murder of
Bishop Juan Gerardi;
Captain Byron Lima Oliva, conspirator in murder of
Bishop Juan Gerardi;
Jose Obdulio Villanueva, conspirator in murder of
Bishop Juan Gerardi;
Rev. Mario Orantes, conspirator in murder of
Bishop Juan Gerardi;

To the fires of silence, the names unknown
except to their families and executioners and ¿Juan quién?
Bishop Juan Gerardi

Bishop Juan Gerardi,
his name is hard to read.

THE TEXAS TEACHER'S COLA

The Texas Teacher says, "Two plus two equals four,
but it would be kind of swell if it equaled five or more,

so Elian could outgrow the Embargo Blues,
return to vote for Florida's family values.

Everything's bigger in Texas, so pour me a tall Coca-Cola,
lite on the coca. Publish my photo sipping and waving 'Hola!'

I need something with a lot of fizz because, gee whiz, 2004
will be here before you know. Vote for me, you're in the door."

Migrant workers who shake his hand stick between his fingers.
Must be all that Coca-Cola that makes them linger.

The Teacher is no generalissimo; he makes people appear.
Mexicanos stare and ask, "Don't we know you from somewhere?"

If enough stick to his fingers when he pulls them from cages,
everyone is happy: he gets votes, they get minimum wages.

"It's like baseball," The Teacher says holding his bat and grin.
"The way we play back in Odessa is three-strikes-I-win."

TESTOSTERONE POISONING:
A MALE PROBLEM

A non-male coworker once told me in a long conversation
over early morning coffee that she looked around the world and saw
men are responsible for more than half the violence.
"It's testosterone surplus," she said.
"All of it oozing around with something to prove."

The rest of my day glared with a milky sheen.
    The video screens in the arcade,
    magazines on the newsstand,
    a candy-apple Ferrari flaunting 90 on 101.
Where it didn't shine, it held us in place like glue:
    on the balcony of the Lambda Chi house at SDSU,
    to the sidewalk across from Scripps Ranch High School,
    in front of the wide-screen at the Belly Up Tavern.

I never agreed entirely with my colleague,
that's why I began to think that we should only cut off
half the balls in the world,
                                        one from each man.

It would slow things down, like taking away a chamber of the heart:
half the honor to defend because
there would be half the balls to challenge it.
Half the unwanted children, half the homeless hard-ons,
half the rapes, half the lonely men with something to prove.

    There was no logic to it, just symmetry:
    What would happen if I upset the ballast of two
    I carry between my legs?
    What if man's soul doesn't reside
    in the chambers of the heart but
    in the *doppelganger* sack? Good and evil, love and hate,
    peace and war?

If a man doesn't flinch when he asks a hard question
and gets a straight answer, we say, "He has balls of steel";
and if he cowers, goes where his woman tells him,
when she tells him, then we say, "He has no balls."
This is wisdom as old as campfires; however,
what I know for truth is my balls are delicate:
a skin marked with veins in the pattern of a spider's web
holds them close to my body on cold mornings.
They feel best when I trust another person to touch them.
Teen nights without sleep they ached.
Now, while making love with my wife, her hand holding
my balls like two eggs,
I've thought about all the reasons she has
to rip them off my God damned body and
heave them into the brush
   where the local coyote could sniff them out
   and run off chewing on the tough nuggets.

If she rid me of just one,
would we get along?
But what if she ripped off the wrong one?
The first Russian doctor into the bunker in Berlin in '45
noted that the charred corpse had only one ball.
Nazi's have always dismissed this as communist propaganda.
Nevertheless, the question remains: if Hitler had both balls,
how many more Jews and Poles and Gays and French and
   Belgians would have died,
the question of balls being significant,
violence being a trait of men
      (according to my non-male friend, it's "simple statistics")?
I must wonder: was Hitler merely running half-speed or
   did he lose the wrong ball?

Sometimes a good cut can't save a life.
Few people know that Jeane Kirkpatrick was born a boy before
she became U.N. Ambassador and friend to the contra in Honduras.
While the OB stitched,
Jeane, who had been set under the heat lamp,
grabbed the scalpel still damp from the episiotomy.
The first slash took the nurse on the back of the hand;
and the second pass left a vertical slice inside her forearm.

Jeane's behavior in the delivery room was so brutal that
her mother requested castration for the safety
                              of the other infants in the nursery.
In the waiting room, the father was told, "It's a girl,"
a shortsighted solution as many acts of desperation are.

Today, if you look at Kirkpatrick's face carefully,
you will see how she resembles John Carradine in good weather.
Even Carradine, horror film star and witness to many gory scenes,
could not watch
      Kirkpatrick's contra brigade in Jinotega
      fill a Sandinista's mouth
      with his own genitalia.
Would it do any good to tell Kirkpatrick's namesakes
that the left ball is for collective effort
and the right ball holds individual strength?

Many causes call for donations, but I have decided
I need both balls,
not just a salmon between my legs
but weight to carry, arrive and leave with,
a load that keeps me from veering off to the left or right
and walking in circles.

SILENT HOURS 1983-1990

In front of the college library, we stood in a line,
several feet apart every Wednesday from noon to one,
gaps between us so others could pass through
like waves rolling past the pilings of a pier,

an hour not of righteous silence but of meditation before
the rest of our week writing letters against wars in Central America.
Streams of rhetoric careened through the blood;
my brain would barrel truth at the deaf,
would shotgun the facts except for one hour that
my closed mouth held the breath of peace.

Someone could see us standing in that silent vigil
and take us for lazy, an hour we could have spent studying.
We did not blockade like S. Brian Willson who gave his legs on the tracks.
I prayed for everyone standing and every one walking, but
what did we want? La paz y la justicia were the words on my lips.
What would they would look?

> One by one people would stand beside us until a line
> stretched south across borders. We would all stand
> praying for peace, thinking about what it would look like—
> drought, pollution, overpopulation, economic disparity—
> the storms of history calm.
>
> Then someone's stomach would rumble,
> someone else would cough, a sick man would faint.
> Someone would leave the line for medicine,
> someone for food, someone to protect his food and medicine,
> and it would start over slowly.

We stood vigil on Wednesday
taking the communion of atrocities and tinkering with broken treaties,
trying to close the gaps between us all.
I sometimes prayed for a world without me in it,
in many ways, a better world, but I couldn't walk away.

ELECTION NIGHT, SAN JUAN DEL SUR, NICARAGUA

February 26, 1990

On the plaza at midnight, party members
repack crates of Victoria cervesa, dump ice
into the gutter: one of many concessions.

Beyond the broken volcanic wall of the bay,
a tiburón swings her tail
and feels tired in history.

Desired justice and justified desire.
Oh, revolution is a Spring Tide.
Tonight the water rolled so far out
I barely hear waves gasping when we stop talking,
wrap ourselves in campaign banners and
lay down on the porch of the National Telephone Office.
A compañero practices throwing his knife into the planked porch floor.

In the morning Ortega comes on T.V. to stop minds from spinning.
We stand still while he circles in the pool of lights.
The water chummed with the blood of martyrs
                                                            and mercenary money,
but he never flashes teeth in the lights on the rostrum.
He looks every night of his forty-four years as
he turns from live microphones dangled before him
and walks into the Managua morning.

POEM IN BLACK AND WHITE

> *The ... classification of colours does not entirely accord with the theories of modern science: Complete lists of shades are beyond the scope of this work —Roget's Thesaurus*

On a December afternoon so cold it would snow
if the sky over Palomar weren't so dry,
we move around to keep ourselves warm:
run the mower back and forth over the umber grass
and believe that it will grow back. But for today
we natives want snow, while the snowbirds from
Chicago and Montreal tell us, "You don't know
what you're asking for."
                                        We want snow to fall on
last Spring's ferns and hush their rustling,
to cover the autumn montage of leaves from
white oaks and sycamores that pile high,
to hold the pages still and whiteout all
but the wet, black trunks that stand up
through the heavy white.
                                        We want the snow to fall and
cushion the rocks and gorse bushes and
leave nothing but the reaching trees. But the
snowbirds tell us, "Only fools wish for snow."

Why would we want a black and white movie, when
under the blue sky we have the florid fallen leaves,
and beneath Palomar, green fairways?
                                                        We try to describe snowy light
cooling our eyes, and the brittle click of stones in our dry summers,
dry like Chicago doesn't understand. We seem to have a drought of words
to make them hear how we need the water, and
how our sunny weather can sustain only so many streams, only
so many towns where the chief joy is not having to shovel snow,
how subtly ceanothus fades from purple to gray in March, and
that gray is a color.

SONS

The son I didn't want
waits until I sit on the bank
before running downhill and jumping on my back.
He waits for me to take indefensible positions,
finds me lying on my back in the living room,
listening to music, falls on my chest and says,
"My eyes are most like yours, aren't they?"

After his older brothers, I lost time,
stayed awake for two years writing my thesis
and signing student loan checks over to my wife.
I wasn't ready for another son
and told her so. I reasoned that
if my father couldn't raise one son,
I could complain about having three.
She listened, then scheduled a vasectomy
at the pregnancy clinic where she volunteered.

He crawls into our bed every night.
Insecure, I think. Does he know
something his brothers don't?
Mornings, I rise sore from sleeping cramped
on the bed's edge, without covers,
stretch my back and legs to shuffle
down the hallway to piss bitterly.

I'd never say I had a favorite,
but I have dreamed about him:
we are both five,
running between rows of orange trees.
Women call our names at the edge of the grove,
but they do not come looking among the trees.

I love him because he is like me:
unwanted, hanging around the neck.
Yet I know he'll let go
when he's ready. I pick him up,
throw him high, hold him by the ankles,
then roll him like a sack of apples across my shoulders,
let him climb me like a tree while I pray
the branches don't break for a boy doesn't soon forget
the moment when pressure against the fingertips
releases except for his own squeezing dry wood
in the moment before the ground makes itself known.

He sits in the boughs
as the wind comes up.
I tell him to come down, but
he laughs until a gust from the arroyo
takes flakes of bark onto the rushing air.
I climb and straddle the limb beside him,
and we're swaying, scared together.

SUBURBAN COWBOYS

The cowboys all left,
rode into the sunset until
they floated on the Pacific while
children watched from streetcorners.

Today's cowboys wear belt buckles
big enough to stop bullets. Just
ask the one in the lavender chaps.
He nods his mint green Stetson, "Yup,"
and around an arena trots his
horse with neck bridled, bowed and lowered,
more like a merry-go-round than a mustang,
or like time-share condos
over-looking waves on the Western Frontier.

HOW TO WRITE WEST

If a white man writes West,
he must write until he comes to the Pacific Ocean,
preferably it will be sunset.

It will be an orange sunset with clouds
and there will be men and women walking hand-in-hand,
like in a catalog but with less light on the clothes.

Turning his eyes back to the sunset,
he'll write "sunset" and not "an optical phenomenon caused by
sunlight through dust and smoke around the spinning earth."

The edge of the land and the edge of the sea
will cut into his mind, the two moving edges.
He'll keep the condominiums to his back and look

at the moving edges no one can own.
If he writes West, he will not notice the erosion
under his feet, at least not on the first night.

But if he returns to watch enough "sunsets" and waves,
and if he sees in detail, he can count the tides and grains of sand.
He might wonder where they go. Once

you wonder where the sand goes and the world starts in motion,
you might feel the need to hold onto the edge of the flat world.
The word "sunset" will dissolve in your mouth like a drug.

You see, the sun never sets,
the world turns away, turns to the east.
Or maybe you're a woman who doesn't believe in hearts

that break. Instead, you believe it is a furnace
pumping warmth through the tower of the body, and
you know the heart does not break, is not sweet and

grows cold only once never to warm again, that no one
enters the tower except by being inhaled or swallowed,
that the windows of eyes and ears don't open to poison us unless

the storms in our minds rage out of control,
the two dark clouds of the brain bumping together
not from the breeze of our breathing but

from the harsh wind of the world that
rushes through the broken glass of eyes staring at the sun and
ears listening to distorted voices insist that the sun sets.

The world tries to help us with its turning,
but our eyes won't orbit; we listen with pounding ears.
Our bodies break from the inside-out.

We stand facing west like towers and believe
our steady gaze is some kind of strength, as
if we could grow roots if we could just hold still.

LAUGHTER PATH

If I lie down for the wheel of time
to roll over me, I am full of use;
I keep time from falling; I catch memories
and hold words as sand holds the colors of
a mandala. Everyday on the beach,
blueprints to circumvent suffering are thrown
and then withdrawn to the laughter of waves.
I remember selling plasma—
the similar salinity of seawater and blood—
my cool red cells flowing back into the vein,
the temperature of my strange self
on the path through my heart.

FIREWORKS

After the wildfire, beneath acres of ash,
the burls wait, fists clutching the oil
            of ceanothus,
                        greasewood,
                                    buckwheat,
waiting to slip their leaves back into the sunlight,
to make lights of their own,
secrets that won't stay underground.

One burl survived our driveway
and split the asphalt, cracked a map for
seeds to fall in and follow the chaparral back.
The manzanita in the rare rain is so red,
the fingers of a thief opening in flames.

Something in me would smell the smoke
and know the invasion needs burning:
            the Russian thistles,
                        tamarisk bushes,
                                    vines of Spanish goat-heads;
something in me would sit still while a Santa Ana carries
sparks like winking eyes of party crashers
from the fire front onto the roof of my house.

The padres ended the traditional burning of sage,
limited incense to censers. Was God praised
when indigenous grasses disappeared from creation?
There's something American about fire and
the faith that somewhere grass seeds wait to split.
Out in the chaparral, a garden without water,
the fuel is piling up, bristling for one lightning strike
for independence.
            We would kill what needs our fiery hands,
                        survives by giving itself to flame,
                                    reminds us how far we still are from home.

INVISIBLE POEM

Poetry makes nothing happen.—W.H. Auden

The poem at the end of his pen
cannot distract his memory as a bottle of rum will,
even if he encloses her curses in quotes
and lights a cigar with the pages to celebrate.
The poem at the end of his pen
is not a knife to slit puncture wounds,
so the venom will drain from his arm.
Were he to jab the pen into the hand of his enemy
whom he loves,
the poem written in her blood
would only reach her heart and
never the circle shadows
behind her forehead,
between her legs,
behind her solar plexus,
between the discs of her spine.
The poem at the end of his pen
gives him no sacred powers
over his wife's lover
even if he sketches
the arc of the man's strut,
the line of the man's hair,
the shape of the man's mouth
when smiling.

The poem at the end of his pen
    stays there, or
the poem at the end of his pen
    is translated into a dozen languages
    that she never learns, or
the pen scratches out pages,
    and he pretends they are her eyes but
    knows they're just surfaces.
She reads this poem
    and doesn't care,
    doesn't remember a line,
    doesn't remember the word "pen,"
    asks, "Was that a poem?"

Part IV: Roots & Limbs

WRITING BY LIGHTNING

After Remington's "Stampede by Lightning"

After inventing Cuban battles for Hearst's newspapers,
Remington painted cattle hurtling right to left with
a horse in the foreground, all four hooves off the ground,
suspended the moment one jagged bolt from the top-right frame
taps the prairie floor,
the horse and electricity trading places.

The cowboy leans forward in his stirrups,
on the same run as the herd
only faster to ride out ahead and turn them right,
bring them back on themselves.
He runs with them but at the edge.

If I were this cowboy, the tallest point on the prairie,
I would lean low over the horse's neck and run, cursing the
real danger, not from lightning, but from the herd
trampling their own.
If I were this cowboy,
I might not want to turn them to the right—
I might let them run wide left beyond the frame—
I might not want to come between the herd and Hearst's artist,
his easel set up on the prairie, painting by lightning.

DREAMING AMERICAN

Trying not to be the white ring around the sun,
I circle slowly like a raven over Mt. Soledad
where you sing down the sky.

The man thinks a disguise of beads and weavings,
but I think otherwise, and being like a raven,
I want to call out but have the voice of adobe bricks stacking.

On this morning after a winter storm,
let your eyes follow my turn away from the Pacific;
you'll see the Cuyamacas rise higher than I can fly.

I listen to your words that would make a man fall from the sky,
so I try to be a raven to follow your sound
east to Tempe or Albuquerque,
into the desert where you will work your life
like an olla, the mouth pouring the precious water
from the cool, quiet dark into the dry light.
I would be the man who waits with
the patience of a boulder in the golden desert light for
water to bring out the flecks of mica in my skin.

One world slams into the other so hard.
I can hear the rumbling from the quarry
and under the river's surface. In the Next World,
I want your voice to crease this desert where we know
who we are, and a black freeway
hisses east to west, and we love nevertheless.

INGRID BERGMAN AT SEA

As a girl, I dreamed in black & white
about the water between islands,
water without current
that held me up as it must have held Jesus.
I didn't walk but lay, gliding my arms and legs
over the surface, making water angels.

I lost my body twice:
the first time to my child,
which cost me the love of my fans.
I did not regret the trade, but
the second time, I lost my body
to itself, the cells multiplying,
still giving birth to me,
my body born twenty-four times per second.
I saw myself from below the water,
floating, the huge wings of the waves I birthed
breaking against the islands and falling back.

"So many beautiful waves," they said
before turning inland. And I regret them all,
every cycle, every reproduction of
my body that flickers without me.
Every frozen frame that won't thaw.
I cannot have them back;
they don't disappear.

SLIDING FROM SEEDS

In the windbreak along the avocado grove,
pomegranates brush against the coyote's fur,
forgotten even by him as he trots through the bushes and
puts his paws on the low limbs to reach the lobes of golden green.
The red globes not as shiny as Christmas bulbs.
Their peels split in ecstasy to show hundreds of bloody teeth.
Ah, how they stain the Santa Ana winds.
Don't deny the juice and leave pomegranates
on the branches for crows or watch the bartender
pour grenadine ribbons in a tequila sunrise.
Taste the juice as it slides from the fiery seed,
let your mouth gape with the bloody rain from its kiss.

COMMENTS ON A STACK OF FIRST DRAFTS

From the sky over my desk,
the paragraphs are lakes;
letters are ripples.
Here's an essay on the people's will:
a calm surface over the mud.
In another on historical silence,
sentence variations drift by like
strands of feathery algae. I float,
a bass in the shadows, and
look for the facts: big fish eats
little fish. A minnow darts between reeds;
I swirl but let him go, leave
a wake of comments in the margins.
Schools of examples turn parallel, sparkle,
then disappear into dim citations.
I'm not really hungry. I'm watching for
a bright back breaking the surface,
mouth open for a blue dragon fly.
We leap to where we can't breathe,
so when we dive deep we know
we're not drifting but swimming.

THE CONFERENCE

"About your poem, it's good
as far as it goes, the car and
all the people," she told me.

"Where could it go?" I asked.
Though my time was nearly
gone, we knew I had two

minutes more before
her next student. "In
the bad old days,

we would say that
it is 'hollow' in the
Hemingway way."

I picked up her words and
listened for the fullness
of my heart, the relentless

rushing of blood throughout
my body; instead I found
the hollow sound of my blood

flowing across my ear drum,
not two beats, but a snare
rolling hollow beneath skin.

After the conference, I thumped
the cage of my ribs that hold
my full heart and my hollow

lungs. Perhaps literature is not
as someone said, "opening a vein and
bleeding on a page," bringing

the inside to the outside.
Perhaps literature is breathing
and escaping the cage, so

the hollowness we hear
is the resonant distance
between my voice and your ear.

COILING

The essay's line of reasoning
blends with ripples of sand
on dunes of paragraphs,

grainy waves with no shore to break on,
just rollers that slap against the right margin.
The dust of summary shifts and rises.

But between the lines and crossing them,
an idea winds with a rattlesnake's purpose.
My eyes follow this other line

that carries power in its jaws,
trail it for a closer look at its design,
knowing it can coil and strike if it needs.

THE CREATURE'S STITCHES

In his basement study, the writer walks
around pages scattered on the floor
and reads until he straddles what could be a first line.
He scratches his left leg but can't find the itch,
a struggle to reconcile what he feels with what he sees.
He closes his eyes to finger the scar where
his right arm was sown together. The memory arcs
to nowhere. On the desk the computer drive whirs,
"We're waiting." His hands—are they his?—
will not stitch a sentence, so he groans.
The wife upstairs yells, "Either come to bed or be quiet."

He considers French kissing the electrical outlet
to prime himself for writing revisions all night—
yum, fresh pages for breakfast—
and catches a moan before it rumbles past his lips.

The manuscript clings to his mind like a bandage to be changed.
His eyes watch the fingers hover over the keys, matches ready to
drop and strike. His eyes watch and wait, afraid to see a flame rise.

ART V. FACT

In English river mud, a statue waits
for archeologists to find below
the humming waters and to excavate
a lioness in stone about to swallow
a man's skull. Perfect: no scratch, no crack,
no sign of empires falling through silt
to magma. Curators wash away the black,
restoring Rome alongside chairs of gilt.

In India, lost jewel of empires,
a box of Ghandi's ashes was found inside
a vault. They gave his fasts' remains to fire,
to river currents, then the ocean tide.
Vermilion faces sang to river stones
while emerald Ghanges took the dust of bones.

RIVER MURMUR

Inside my chest curls a river I've never followed.
You wait onshore somewhere upstream.
Which bank of the river, I do not know.
I hear you talking.
To whom do your words belong?
Follow a leaf on the current of this poem.
I will wait down river, and when I see you coming,
I will swim over.
We'll stand in the shallows
    over the sandbar;
    green reeds will shade us;
    this poem will shine over you.
You have set whatever fire consumes this page.
These letters sway and arc from your hair.

Night writes with dark words,
    behind the sun's light.
I often lie awake without you and say your name,
the murmur in this poem.

When I run, I'm singing.
Follow the rising of my chest.
My river floods its banks.
Move the poem out of my hands.
You have dived into the river with me.

In the water we touch, suspended
    over the sand,
no need to hold our breath and dive.
The current carries us and rushes past.
We hold one another; we drown; we part and swim.

POURING COFFEE

When I pour coffee,
I deal a rush after a heavy meal.
I slide up to the banquet table,
the pot, a black fist.

When I pour coffee,
I rarely have to ask:
you nod;
I move

the mouth of my pot over
the mouth of your cup,
careful not to touch.

The scalding black drops
into the circle of china.
I make it slide down the wall,

so it won't spill.
If I pull back as I fill your cup,
it gives the illusion that I'm taking,

when the truth is a fist drives through the coffee.
This coffee was not ground;
it burst spontaneously at your presence.

Its arm punched out of the Guatemalan earth,
through the burlap and steel and paper and water.
The sip I tasted shakes my heart but not my hand.

As the coffee rises to the rim,
I bring the pot close to your cup so
you can see whatever grounds might be dragged

to the pot's mouth, how I control the flow
and spare you the bitter fragments that
sink back into the coffee that I don't pour.

SAILING FROM MY TONGUE

When I first surrender to a half moon
of watermelon, I take the slice to the lawn.
Red flesh pushes past my lips, dissolves against my
teeth before sliding down my throat.
But at the corners of my mouth, the
juice drips across my jaw and
traces my swallowing down my neck and chest.
If I get sloppy, my navel fills like a cup at a feast.
Sometimes I lean over the rind
and lift my head only after I've filled
my cheeks with seeds that I roll
onto the tip of my tongue
and set spinning and sailing onto the lawn.
Later I hold only the new-moon rind
with its dark-side green,
which I pitch over the trees
while the melon of summer filling my belly
seeps into my dry cells.

THE EMPTYING

after Scott Reid

Nine years ago, I seduced
you with poems though
sometime between then and now
I stopped relying on your opinion. You say
I love metaphor too much, that it is
so much lard slathered onto the poem's drive
like talking with one's mouth full, swallowing
and spitting, so let me say
this on point: I want to clear a place
in our house, as it was when
we first moved in together.
I'm carrying the tchotchke and
bibliotheca out into the sunlight,
leaving dark spaces indoors,
a gift, this house as when
we first discovered it, a mouth,
lips parting for a kiss,
ready to forgo food or
breathing for a moment together.

"SO WHAT"?

to Miles Davis

Turn back.
You make me listen.
Make me listen.
Turn back.

With the glisten
from the stage lights,
blind me.
With your horn-bell's glisten,
blind me.

Let the trumpet
fill the distance.
Turn back.
Fill the distance
with your music.
So what?
You make me listen,
to the beauty.
Now turn,
and make me see.

SOLO TO DOUBLE BARS: ELEGY FOR JACO PASTORIOUS

Jaco, oh Jaco,
never bound to low tones,
you found the harmonics ringing
somewhere between the fretboard and the bridge
of your sunburst Fender Jazz bass,
your main ax later
splintered beside you in the street.

While you played, we listened to
your melodies in rare frequencies:
low tones sharp as electricity,
high tones ethereal as breathing.

We applauded each solo,
slapping our hands together.
Oh Jaco,
you hid some music when
you smashed your guitars
and just left Jaco.

So you came around after hours,
knocking on the door with the soles of you shoes.
You came around empty handed.
    Should we have known then? Or when
    you cut off your long, brown hair? Or
    passed out across the railroad tracks?

At last you made
the front page of *The Times*;
they told us
"He
was
35."
Beaten to death
for erratic behavior,
and so you had played,
and so I had listened.
Oh Jaco,
if the young bassists just tuning-up
had heard you play before
they read of your death,
then they would've heard you
        without the blue:
the hidden machinery's throb and thrust
behind the acetate curtain,
ringing from the range of overtones,
nowhere on the ebony,
but coming back to us.

I listen for you
where I lost you;
every wino I pass
sleeping in the park,
        keeping time in a building's shade or
                slumped on a sidewalk pillow,
I wonder if he can play,
        stand up on the street,
                step away from the empty bottle,
                        over the glinting shards and
                                loosen note after note from himself
until
he
lays
a
walking
line
down
Dixie Highway,
        not just straight-ahead,
but with a shuffle for
anticipation,
with a slur in the pattern,

        —fretless—

never just straight ahead
but every now and
then turning for a few steps
the other way... like Jaco.

ON FLYING

Indoors on the beam bisecting the window,
        the junco paced and flounced.
Did it press for the mountain or
        fly against the bird mirrored outdoors?
From where did the jagged words come fluttering
        against this window's page?

My neighbor Gary stood on a stool
        and the bird flew up many times before
collapsing into his hands, which he offered to me.
        I clasped my hands over his.
The wings brushed my calloused palms.
        Someone watching at that moment might have thought we
        were praying the same prayer.
The jagged feet reached for something to wrap around.
        It felt good to walk outside and
open my palms to the mountain.

That afternoon we played baseball and
        I imbued every throw with
the momentum of survival the bird left beneath my skin.
        I flew at every ball, hoped to catch even Gary's hits,
play off the diamond's mirrored angles,
        catch the out, take the bat and
release a pitch into flight.

BENEATH THE COVERS

after Harwood's "In the Park"

Our mother presents us like evidence at trial
for her old lover, to show him how this road often taken
has given her joy and made her life awaken.
The poor man does all he can not to smile
too much. What could he know that we don't? As lovers,
children are the most intimate. We see past beauty,
if we see it at all, to the flaws, to the pain of duty.
We clean our rooms, wash up and wait between the covers.

In the sand at her feet I scratch lines to form the pattern
of the possible lives they could live from today on.
See, on this planet all lines intersect if we follow
them far enough. Our poor mother bets all on her children,
believing we are more faithful than lovers though we abandon
her a day at a time. She is an egg we split and leave hollow.

Part v: Through Windows

THE WAY BETWEEN US

Beside a Torreya Pine on a ridge,
my son Keaton points out
where someone left her red fingerprint on a brown bird's wing.
Keaton follows the bird around the trail to another ridge while
mosquitoes rise out of the canyon like smoke from a fire.
The gorge between us, I stand by the pine to study
a cocoon caught in a cobweb between green needles.
On Sunday afternoons, my grampy napped in a hammock,
before throwing himself into the jaws of Monday.
I, too, gave up my oak with its shade,
often left for work and arrived home in the dark.
But like a logging road cut through the forest,
there is a way between us, though it isn't the only way.
Tonight we will sleep on the ground,
Keaton and I looking at the stars
through the pine lace.

FARSIGHTED HUSBAND SPEAKS

I started calling you "Darlin'" when
we were 16 in high school and James Taylor sang,
"Oh, Darlin', Darlin', is that the way you look?"

In history class I missed the causes for the Civil War,
my eyes glancing two rows over to
where you sat in fact reading the page.
How could I have known you were nearsighted?
Oh, what we overlook!
I found myself floating like a balloon above a parade.

Now, with three sons lined up between us,
my orbit has taken me to the opposite end of the dinner table
from you. These other men in your life will leave you
staring after them after they have rounded the curve down the road.

GOD SONG

apologies to John Coltrane

I've been up since the dawn,
listening to the rivers in my veins,
lightning in my brain,
playing along
to that God song.

Fog on the road,
from the sea
every wave His blue breath
coming to me.
Heartbeats break on the shoreline
to that God song.

ICE DRUM

My oldest son and I stand quiet and stare at the snow,
as if we can't believe such cold
could cover a California pond.
I break frozen stones from the silenced stream
and skitter offbeats over the ice.
Could the pond be colder than November when Jesse and I swam
with our bodies flat on the surface where
the sun dove only eight inches deep?

On a dare, we dove for mud:
I held Jesse's hand and pulled him
through deep blue, dark green and into the black
where the pond shut its eye to the sun.
We blew our breath into
the water wrapped around us and
dropped through the dark, cold as January.
The muck so soft we didn't feel it until we were deep.
We grabbed blind handfuls, turned and
kicked toward the remembered light.
Only on the surface did we see the black proof
slipping finely between our fingers.
In wet light, mica reflects sky
and the muck absorbs heat
before slipping back into cold.

Jesse breaks ice sheets from the shore
and slides them over the skin of
the ice drum resonating over
the cold that only dives deeper in June.
Surfaces change and we say nothing as
my stones ping and crack
and his ice hums and sizzles
on this morning when only my first born and I hear this music
back through seasons and
down to the bottom.

End Notes

END NOTES

"Mercy" — This poem was written as vocalese to the Jaco Pastorious' instrumental cover, not knowing Buddy Guy had already written his own lyrics. "So What" and "God Song" were also written as vocaleses.

"God Box" — Connie Chung is a television journalist who fooled former Speaker of the House Newt Gingrich's mother into revealing on camera that her son referred to the First Lady as "that bitch."

"God Acts" — The word *tukwut* (took-woot) is the indigenous word for mountain lion throughout the San Luis Rey River area.

"Guatemalan Fires" — In 1998 Bishop Juan Gerardi, head of the Catholic Church's Human Rights Office in Guatemala, was bludgeoned to death two days after reporting the Guatemalan military – including alumni of the School of the Americas at Fort Benning, Georgia – was responsible for the overwhelming majority of 200,000 deaths in that country's civil war. One of these School of the Americas' alumni was implicated in Gerardi's assassination.

"Writing by Lightning" — Remington's imaginary renderings of Spanish soldiers shooting Cuban peasants were presented as fact in Hearst newspapers and subsequently presented as evidence on the floor of the U.S. Congress as justification to declare war. The sketch's ficticious casualties prompted real ones — an example of art that can kill.

ABOUT THE AUTHOR

Brandon Cesmat currently teaches literature and writing at Cal State University San Marcos and serves on the board of California Poets in the Schools. He is the poet-vocalist in the performance ensemble Drought Buoy. He lives with his wife and three sons — all of whom can kick his butt in Halo, chess and paintball — in Valley Center, California.

ABOUT THE COVER

The cover photo is from David Avalos' installation "The 480-Year-Old Mestizo," a work in wood, mild steel, tempered glass and light inspired by a stolen gardenia, the Codex Duran, and a shipwrecked Spaniard named Guerrero. A social observer and artist provocateur, Avalos engages his audiences in the experience of cultural tradition and change, and public/private codes of behavior from a Chicano perspective.